Oceans

Philip Sauvain

 Carolrhoda Books, Inc. / Minneapolis

All words that appear in **bold** are explained in the glossary that starts on page 30.

Photographs courtesy of: Robert Harding Picture Library / Geoff Renner 22t; The Hutchison Library 28bc; / Bernard Regent 19b, 22b; / Sarah Errington 25; Impact Photos / Alan Blair 28br; NHPA / Norbert Wu 16b; Nova Scotia Power Inc.13t; John R. Patton 19t, 20t; Philip A.Sauvain 9b, 11b, 12, 18, 21; South American Pictures / Tony Morrison 15t; Still Pictures / Ora - cover, 4; / Klein/Hubert - title page; / Mark Edwards 9t, 24t; / Gerard & Margi Moss 11t; / Rafel Al Ma'ary 15b; / Norbert Wu 16t & c, 17; / Heldur Metocny 20b; / John Maier 24b, 27b; / Edward Parker 27t, 28bl; UKAEA 13b.

Illustrations and maps by David Hogg.

This edition first published in the United States in 1996 by Carolrhoda Books, Inc.

A ZOË BOOK

Copyright © 1996 Zoë Books Limited. Originally produced in 1996 by Zoë Books Limited, Winchester, England.

Carolrhoda Books, Inc., c/o The Lerner Group
241 First Avenue North, Minneapolis, MN 55401

Library of Congress Cataloging-in-Publication Data

Sauvain, Philip Arthur.
    Oceans / by Philip Sauvain.
      p. cm. — (Geography detective)
    "A Zoë book" — T.p. verso.
    Includes index.
    Summary: Describes oceans of the world, including the plants, animals, and human use, with case studies of specific areas.
    ISBN 1-57505-043-9 (lib. bdg. : alk. paper)
      1. Oceans — Juvenile literature. [1. Ocean.] I. Title. II. Series.
GC21.5.S28 1997
551.46 — dc20   96-14810
                                           CIP
                                            AC

Printed in Italy by Grafedit SpA.
Bound in the United States of America
1 2 3 4 5 6 02 01 00 99 98 97

Contents

Seas, Oceans, and Coastlines 4

The Shape of the Ocean Floor 6

Water, Water, Everywhere 8

Ocean Currents and Weather 10

Why the Oceans Are Never Still 12

Plants and Animals of the Sea 14

Deep-sea Creatures 16

How Oceans Shape the Land 18

Coastal Hazards 20

Defending the Coastline 22

How We Use Oceans and Seas 24

Poisoning the Water 26

Mapwork 28

Glossary 30

Index 32

Seas, Oceans, and Coastlines

If you were to look at the world from space, the first thing you'd notice is that it seems to be blue. Less than a third of the earth's surface is land. The rest is salt water, stretching its way around the globe. Earth is the only planet that has water on this scale.

▼ Areas of the oceans that are surrounded on two or three sides by land are called **seas**, such as the South China Sea; or **bays**, such as the Bay of Bengal; or **gulfs**, such as the Gulf of Mexico. Seas are smaller and not as deep as the oceans. A few seas, such as the Caspian, are surrounded on all sides by land. A narrow channel of water, called a **strait**, may link one sea to another or to an ocean. The Bering Strait links the Bering Sea to the Arctic Ocean.

▲ In the part of the world shown here, there is far more ocean than land. This ratio is typical of much of the earth's surface.

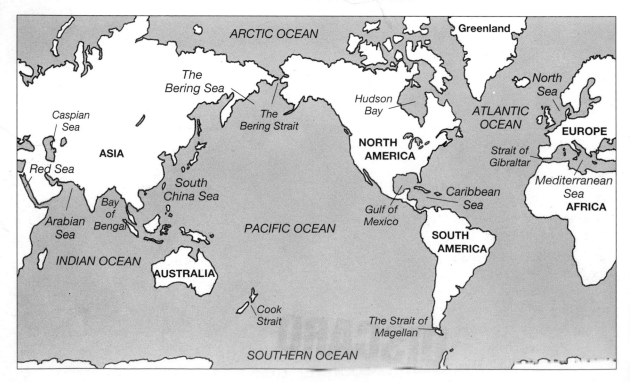

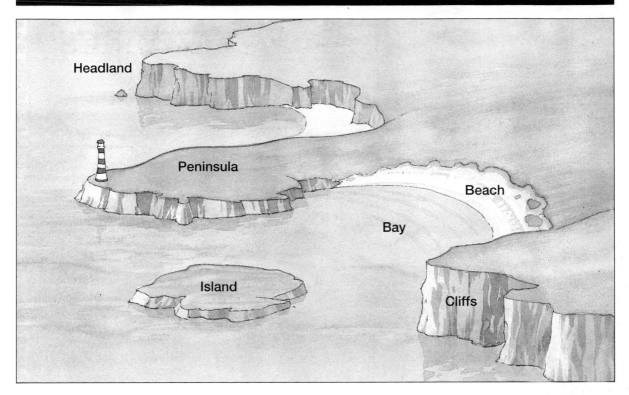

The continents split the water into four main oceans. North and South America separate the Pacific Ocean from the Atlantic. Africa, Asia, and Australia encircle the Indian Ocean, separating it from the Pacific and the Atlantic. The fourth ocean, the ice-bound Arctic at the North Pole, is much smaller than the others. It is surrounded by Alaska, northern Canada, Greenland, and northern Russia.

▲ Coastlines define the edges of the seas and oceans. This drawing shows how the sea has shaped coastal features in different ways. A **headland**, for example, is a small piece of high land that sticks out into the sea. A **peninsula** is a much larger piece of land that stretches out into the water. *Peninsula* means "almost an island" in Latin.

● To the north of the **equator**, there is one-and-a-half times as much water as land. To the south of it, there is four times as much water as land.

● The Pacific Ocean (70 million square miles) is O-shaped. It is nearly twice the size of the S-shaped Atlantic Ocean (36 million sq mi).

● The Pacific is so big that you could place all the land on the earth's surface there and still have room for a second Asia — the largest continent — as well.

● The Indian Ocean (29 million sq mi) is shaped like an upside-down V. It is nearly as big as the Atlantic. The O-shaped Arctic Ocean is much smaller (3.6 million sq mi).

Geography Detective

Look at a map of your country. Note the seas and oceans that surround it. Write down the name of the island nearest to your home. Which is the nearest: a) ocean, b) sea, c) bay, d) gulf, e) strait, f) peninsula?

5

The Shape of the Ocean Floor

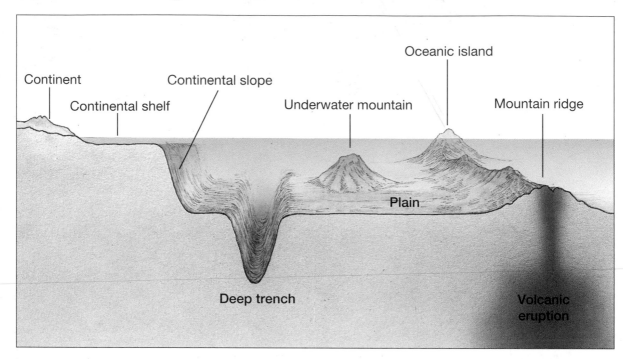

Continent

Continental shelf

Continental slope

Underwater mountain

Oceanic island

Mountain ridge

Plain

Deep trench

Volcanic eruption

The drawing opposite shows what an ocean would look like without water. The **ocean bed**, or floor, is like a huge basin. In it there are channels, or **trenches**, that are deeper than the rest of the floor. Long lines of mountains and **volcanoes** rise from the ocean bottom, sometimes piercing the surface of the water to form islands. At the edges of the ocean, a steep incline called the **continental slope** separates the ocean bed from the more shallow seabed around the continents. The area nearest to the land is the **continental shelf**, where the water is not more than about 650 feet deep.

People who study the earth are called geologists. Most geologists believe that more than 200 million years ago, there were two huge landmasses on earth. Smaller landmasses broke away from these to form continents. The continents slowly moved apart, leaving the ocean basins in between. The Indian Ocean, for example, was formed when the continents of Antarctica and Africa moved apart.

▲ Take a look at a section of a typical ocean. Notice the continental shelf close to the land. This area is where most fish are caught, and where oil is taken from the seabed.

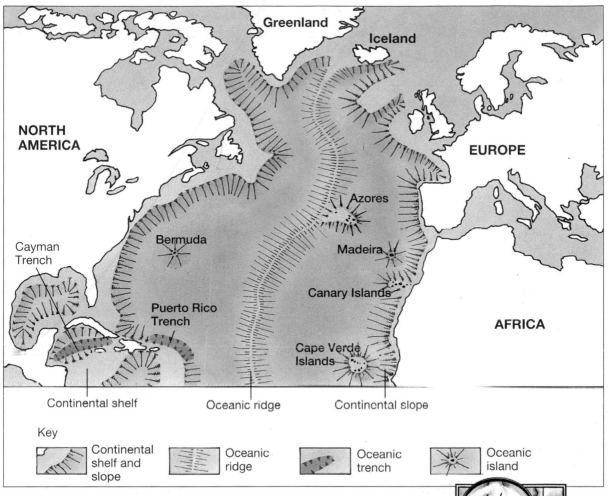

Greenland

Iceland

NORTH AMERICA

EUROPE

Cayman Trench

Bermuda

Azores

Madeira

AFRICA

Puerto Rico Trench

Canary Islands

Cape Verde Islands

Continental shelf   Oceanic ridge   Continental slope

Key

| | Continental shelf and slope | | Oceanic ridge | | Oceanic trench | | Oceanic island |

▲ This map of the North Atlantic Ocean shows the mountains, long ridges, and deep trenches of the ocean bed. Some of the mountains rise above the surface, forming islands such as Madeira and Bermuda.

Geography Detective

Trace the outline of South America from the map on page 4. Cut out the shape you've traced and move it around on the map so that it fits neatly against the coastline of Africa. There will be one or two small gaps but you should be able to see how the land fit together millions of years ago. Which ocean was formed when the two continents moved apart?

● On average, the world's oceans are over two miles deep. That is about twenty times as deep as the average sea.

● The deepest part of the Pacific Ocean, the Mariana Trench east of the Philippine Islands, is nearly seven miles deep.

● Mauna Kea (13,796 feet) and Mauna Loa (13,677 feet) are volcanoes on the island of Hawaii in the middle of the Pacific Ocean. The ocean bed from which the island has grown is 19,680 feet deep.

● If all the water in the Pacific dried up, Mauna Kea would be the world's highest mountain. Its combined height of 33,476 feet (13,796 feet above water; 19,680 feet below) makes it even higher than Mount Everest (29,028 feet).

Water, Water, Everywhere

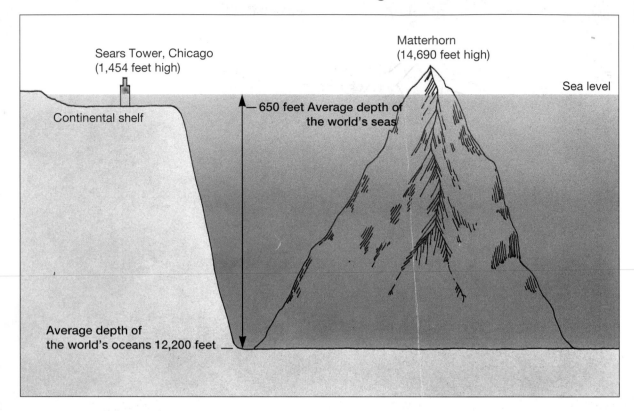

Sears Tower, Chicago
(1,454 feet high)

Matterhorn
(14,690 feet high)

Sea level

Continental shelf

— 650 feet Average depth of
the world's seas

Average depth of
the world's oceans 12,200 feet —

▲ The average depth of the ocean is 12,200 feet. This is deep enough to cover all of Europe, apart from the tops of its highest mountains, such as the Matterhorn (14,690 feet). By contrast, if Chicago's 1,454-foot-high Sears Tower, one of the world's tallest buildings, were moved to the continental shelf, much of it would be above sea level.

Seawater is very salty to taste. It contains salt and other solids from the land. These materials have been washed into the sea by rivers. (Some solids have dissolved in the water, which is why you cannot see them.) The solids in the water make it easier for swimmers and boats to float.

On average, seawater is 3.5 percent salt. In some places, people make shallow channels, or salt pans, to hold seawater and collect salt. Gradually the water evaporates, or dries up, leaving behind the salt.

● The world's seas and oceans hold 329 billion cubic miles of water. This amount would give each person on earth enough water to fill 50,000 large swimming pools!

● Seawater contains very tiny quantities of many substances other than salt, such as magnesium, sulfur, and even gold.

● The amount of gold in seawater is tiny. But because there is so much water, the total weight of gold in the sea is more than a hundred times greater than that of all the gold ever mined in the world.

◀ The women in this picture are collecting salt from salt pans near Hambantota, Sri Lanka.

Freshwater can also be made from salt water. When salt water evaporates, the salt is left behind and the water turns into a gas. This gas, or water vapor, can be trapped in a tank and cooled. Cooling turns the vapor back into water, but without salt in it. This is a very expensive way of making freshwater that only rich countries can afford. Factories that make freshwater are called **desalinization plants**. Several plants sit along the desert coasts of the Middle East, in Kuwait and Saudi Arabia, where supplies of freshwater are very low.

▶ Some sea creatures, such as coral, have hard skeletons. They make their skeletons out of solids they take from the seawater. Shellfish, like those shown here, use tiny amounts of a substance called calcium to make their shells.

Geography Detective

Find two large jars of the same size. Call them A and B. Fill them halfway with water, then stir half a cupful of salt into jar A. Take a small jar or tall cup that will fit inside the two large jars. Put it into jar A and pour water into it. Stop pouring when the jar is about to sink. Now lift the inner jar of water and put it carefully into jar B. What happens to it? What does this tell you about the water in jars A and B?

Ocean Currents and Weather

The winds that blow across the oceans often bring rain and sometimes snow. A wind that blows mainly from one direction is called a prevailing wind. Prevailing winds help to form **ocean currents**. Currents are great streams of seawater that move through the ocean. For example, the Gulf Stream carries warm water from the Gulf of Mexico across the North Atlantic Ocean. This current warms the shores of western Europe and keeps the seas there free from ice in winter. Other currents, such as the Peru Current off the coast of South America, are cold. They bring cooler weather. When the warm Gulf Stream meets the cold Labrador Current off the coast of Canada, thick fog forms.

The sun's heat causes rapid water evaporation over warm seas near the equator. The water vapor collides with winds from different directions and rises to form a towering column of fast-moving air. When this happens, **hurricanes** can quickly form.

● If there were no oceans to warm the earth, the weather would be far too cold for human life to survive.

● A hurricane is called a cyclone in many places, such as India. In eastern Asia people call it a typhoon.

● People have named some hurricanes and typhoons such as Andrew, Beatrice, and Christine. These names make it easier to record how and where the storms are moving.

▼ The areas that are most at risk from hurricanes are shown on this world map. Blue and red arrows show the main ocean currents.

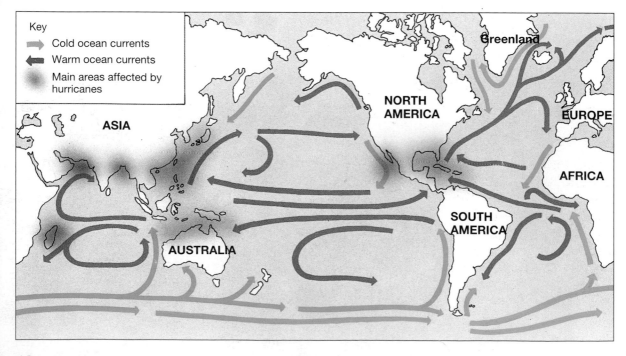

Key
➡ Cold ocean currents
⬅ Warm ocean currents
Main areas affected by hurricanes

ASIA
NORTH AMERICA
EUROPE
AFRICA
SOUTH AMERICA
AUSTRALIA
Greenland

A hurricane sweeps through Apia, the capital of Western Samoa, on the island of Upolu in the Pacific Ocean.

Hurricanes can move at speeds of up to 200 miles per hour, destroying everything in their paths. The storms are terrifying for people on land as well as for ships at sea.

Case Study

The worst hurricane in recent years killed 140,000 people in Bangladesh in April 1991. The storm swept in from the Bay of Bengal at a speed of 144 miles per hour. Many people and animals drowned when low-lying farmland flooded. Residents were warned about the hurricane, but many were afraid to leave their farms and animals. More than five million people lost their homes in the floods. Numerous fishing boats disappeared at sea.

This subtropical tree is growing on the coast of northwestern Scotland. Trees like this typically grow much farther south. They are able to grow in this part of Scotland because the Gulf Stream brings mild temperatures to the area. In other places this far north, the sea usually freezes in winter.

Geography Detective

What damage can a hurricane cause to a town? Why are hurricane warnings important in places such as Florida and Japan? What can people do to prevent hurricane damage in towns?

Why the Oceans Are Never Still

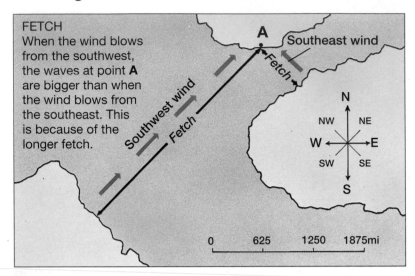

FETCH
When the wind blows from the southwest, the waves at point **A** are bigger than when the wind blows from the southeast. This is because of the longer fetch.

Southeast wind

Fetch

Southwest wind

Fetch

N
NW   NE
W ← → E
SW   SE
S

0   625   1250   1875mi

◀ Waves usually move toward the coast at an angle. The distance they travel uninterrupted across the sea is called the **fetch**. The longer the fetch is, the more powerful the waves.

▲ Waves crashing on a rocky shore

The oceans are never still. Their currents are always moving, carrying water from one part of the world to another. Oceans are also never still because the action of the wind causes waves to form on the surface. The stronger the wind and the longer it blows, the bigger the waves. Waves also increase in size when they travel across a long stretch of water.

At most places along the coast, the level of the sea rises twice a day at high **tide** (the flood tide) and falls back at low tide (the ebb tide). High tides can raise the level of the water at the coast by as much as 50 feet. Tides are caused by the force of gravity from the sun and the moon, which pull the water toward them, much like a magnet. At the times of the full and the new moons each month, the sun and the moon are in line with one another and with the earth. Their joint pull is at its strongest, causing the highest tides, or **spring tides**. In between, twice each month when the sun, the moon, and the earth are positioned like the corners of a triangle, the tides are at their lowest. These are the **neap tides**.

● For fishermen, who rely on high water to sail in and out of harbors, the high tides indicate the beginning and the end of the work day. This schedule is observed around the world.

▲ Engineers have found ways to use the power of rising and falling tides to produce electricity. This tidal power station is on the Annapolis River in Nova Scotia, Canada. It is positioned where the river runs into the Bay of Fundy. A 50-foot difference between high and low tide levels occurs in the bay. The moving tide water turns the blades of the turbines in the power station.

Case Study

Since the 1970s, people have experimented with capturing and using the power of waves. Engineers are now trying out a wave-powered station off the northern coast of Scotland. The facility is called the Osprey, after a type of sea eagle. The Osprey is over 70 feet high and is anchored to the seabed. With a hollow center, it looks something like a cave with a tower on top. On either side of the central "cave" is a barrier that directs the waves into the cave's entrance. As the waves rush in and out of the space, the water pushes air up and sucks it back down. The up and down movement of the air turns machines called turbines inside the tower. The turbines help generate electricity.

▶ The Osprey wave-powered station

Geography Detective

You can see how the wind forms waves by doing this simple experiment at home. Fill a sink or basin with cold water. Blow lightly across the water. What do you notice? What happens if you blow harder or closer to the water? What happens when you stop blowing? Is there a difference between blowing a short distance across the basin and blowing along the whole length of the basin?

Plants and Animals of the Sea

Thousands of different plants and animals live in the sea. Most reside in the shallow waters of the continental shelf or in the upper layers of ocean water. The sun warms these waters. **Phytoplankton**, tiny plantlike organisms that live near the surface, cannot exist without sunlight. Another type of **plankton** is an animal called **zooplankton**. Most kinds of plankton are so small that scientists need a microscope to study them.

- The sea contains more than 200,000 different types, or species, of plants and animals.
- Ocean species range in size from huge whales, up to 100 feet long, to plants and creatures so small they cannot be seen without a powerful microscope.

▼ Plants and animals of the sea can be categorized according to where they live. Read more about the creatures that live in the ocean deeps on pages 16 and 17.

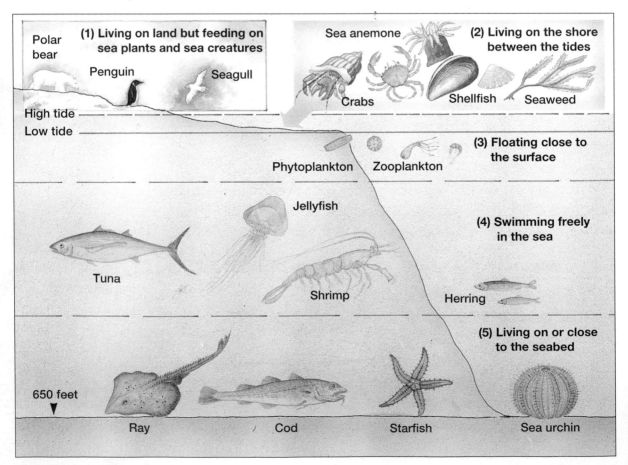

Polar bear

(1) Living on land but feeding on sea plants and sea creatures

Penguin

Seagull

Sea anemone

(2) Living on the shore between the tides

Crabs

Shellfish

Seaweed

High tide

Low tide

Phytoplankton

Zooplankton

(3) Floating close to the surface

Jellyfish

(4) Swimming freely in the sea

Tuna

Shrimp

Herring

(5) Living on or close to the seabed

650 feet
▼

Ray

Cod

Starfish

Sea urchin

Plankton are the basic food of the oceans. Without them, there would be little life in the water. Most zooplankton live by feeding on phytoplankton. Shrimp and small fish eat the zooplankton, while larger fish, such as herring, feed on the small fish and the shrimp. Larger fish still, such as tuna, feed on the herring. Other creatures eat the tuna. And so it goes. A system like this, where creatures are dependent on each other for food, is called a **food chain**, or food web.

▲ Sometimes seawater looks red. Known as red tide, the phenomenon is caused by organisms called dinoflagellates, which contain a poison. The substance doesn't harm the shellfish that feed on dinoflagellates, but if people eat the shellfish, they may die.

◀ A **coral reef** in the Red Sea. The corals, whose skeletons form reefs like this, live in shallow water near the ocean surface.

Geography Detective

Look at this picture of a rock pool. What different types of sea creatures and plants can you see? Where would you expect to find a rock pool like this? (Look at the diagram on page 14). What other forms of wildlife would you look for if you visited a beach?

Deep-sea Creatures

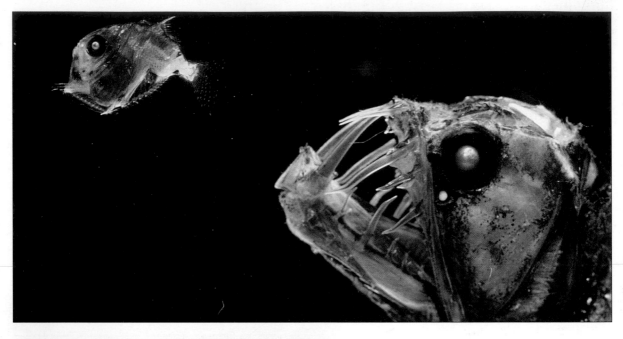

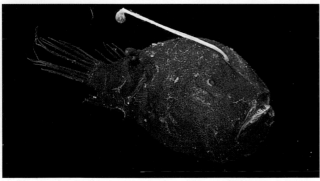

▲ The viper fish here (right) is chasing a hatchet fish deep below the ocean surface.

◄ A part of this fish glows in the dark. This attracts prey that the fish eats.

▼ The gulper eel can swallow fish that have bodies bigger than its own!

Although most sea creatures live in water that is warmed by the sun, some live in the ocean deeps. We know about them from scientists who have explored the ocean floor. One expedition went down nearly seven miles to the deepest part of the Pacific Ocean. Ships that explore the ocean depths are called submersibles. Some of these ships have no crews. Scientists on the surface use computers to control the submersibles. Onboard are strong lights and television cameras, which take pictures of the ocean bed.

Lights are needed because it is very dark in the ocean deeps. The water is also generally very cold — between 37.4°F and 48.2°F. No plants grow in these frigid waters. The creatures that live in the ocean deeps have developed in special ways, enabling them to survive in deep-sea conditions. We call this adaptation to the environment.

Since there is so little light in deep waters, some fish have grown huge eyes to make the best use of the minimal light. At very great depths, where the water is pitch black, the fish are blind. Many deep-sea creatures, such as anglerfish, are luminous. They glow in the dark. The bright glow attracts other, smaller, fish toward anglerfish, which then swallow the small fish whole.

There is also little food at this depth. Most of what there is sinks down from the warmer ocean layers above. Some deep-sea fish have huge mouths with sharp teeth to catch as much food as possible.

- ● Anglerfish have long, sharp teeth that curve backwards towards their throats. Once a fish has been swallowed it cannot escape the anglerfish.
- ● Lantern fish rise to the surface at night to feed on zooplankton. By day they live in the ocean deeps, 3,250 feet below the surface of the sea.

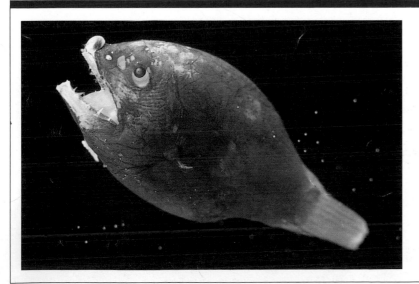

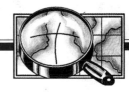

Geography Detective

Draw or trace your own picture of an anglerfish. Draw in arrows and add labels to point to the clues on the fish that tell you: a) that it lives in the ocean deeps where the ocean is very dark; b) there is little food where it lives so it has had to develop a surefire way of catching other creatures.

How Oceans Shape the Land

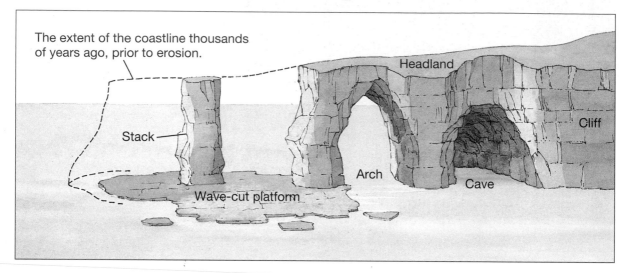

The extent of the coastline thousands of years ago, prior to erosion.

Headland

Cliff

Stack

Arch

Cave

Wave-cut platform

Waves shape the coastlines around the world's seas and oceans. At high tide, they smash against rocks and surge into caves. As they do so, they pick up pebbles from the beach and hurl them at the cliff face. The pebbles hit against other pebbles and rocks, wearing down the edges and making the pebbles round and smooth. The waves also break away bits of rock from cliffs, especially when the rock is loose or softer than the surrounding rocks. In this way, waves can cut holes in the steepest and toughest of cliffs. The bits of rock that the waves wash away will eventually break up into tiny pieces of sand.

The holes in a cliff get bigger and deeper over hundreds of years. Eventually they form caves in the face of the cliff. If they break through to the other side of the cliff, they

▲ This drawing shows how the sea shapes a coastline. The waves have formed a cliff, **stack**, cave, and arch. They also left behind a **wave-cut platform**.

► The large area of bare rock seen here is a wave-cut platform. It is all that is left of the cliffs. The sea eroded this coastline thousands of years ago.

On some lowland coasts, strips of sand or mud, called **sandbars**, form across the entrance to a bay. The bars form when a current carrying sand and mud reaches calmer, deeper water. The sand drops to the seabed. Slowly, it builds up to form a bar. When a sandbar cuts off a bay from the sea, the water forms a **lagoon**. Cape Hatteras, North Carolina, shown here, is a large sand island that sits near numerous sandbars.

create an arch. If the roof of the arch then collapses, it leaves behind a small piece of rock called a stack. A stack stands on its own a few yards away from the cliff.

Underneath the waves the sea is quite calm. This is why the only part of the cliff that the waves wear away, or **erode**, is the strip of rock between low and high tide. The rocks above the high-tide line then collapse, while the rocks below the low-tide mark are left behind. The remaining low rocks form a wave-cut platform, covered with sand, that can be seen at low tide.

● The rocks that the sea cuts away from cliffs break up into pebbles, shingle (large gravel), sand, and mud. These are moved along the shore by the action of the waves, tides, and currents. This action is called **longshore drift**.

● Longshore drift can block up the mouths of rivers. It sometimes forms sandbanks or mud banks close to the shore.

Geography Detective

Look at this photograph. What clues tell you that the waves have shaped the coastline? Make a list of the names of all the features you can see in the picture.

Coastal Hazards

◀ This beach house is on an island off the East Coast of the United States. It has been damaged by big, powerful waves that roll in from the Atlantic Ocean when the winds are especially strong.

The sea usually erodes the coasts very slowly, but erosion can happen quickly as well. Where cliffs are made of soft rocks, the waves may cut them back by 16 to 20 feet each year. Houses and roads may fall into the sea as a result of coastal erosion.

A danger to low-lying coasts, such as those in the Netherlands and Bangladesh, is flooding. This can happen when gales cause high waves at the same time as the highest tides of the month.

● Some of the worst coastal floods are caused by waves called **tsunami**. These waves can be three times as high as a house and can travel as fast as an airplane. They are caused by earthquakes or volcanic eruptions on the seabed. The waves mostly affect the coasts of Japan and other countries that border the Pacific Ocean.

● When the Indonesian volcano of Krakatoa erupted on August 27, 1883, it caused terrifying waves 130 feet high. Thousands of people on the coasts of Java and Sumatra were drowned.

◀ A flooded home in Bangladesh

Sometimes earthen banks, or seawalls, are built to protect the coast from flooding. When waves break these walls, seawater will rush through. The damage can be enormous and people may drown if they cannot escape to higher land. In 1970 a terrible flood killed 150,000 people who lived near the coast in Bangladesh (known then as East Pakistan). A great sea wave swept over the land during a typhoon, drowning people and animals.

On some low-lying coasts, the wind and the waves leave behind deposits of sand and pebbles, and so the coast grows outwards. Towns that were on the coast may now be inland.

Geography Detective

These drawings tell the story of All Saints Church at Dunwich in eastern England. What clue is left today to tell us about this church? Why did the church fall into ruin in the 1800s? Explain what happened at Dunwich, and why.

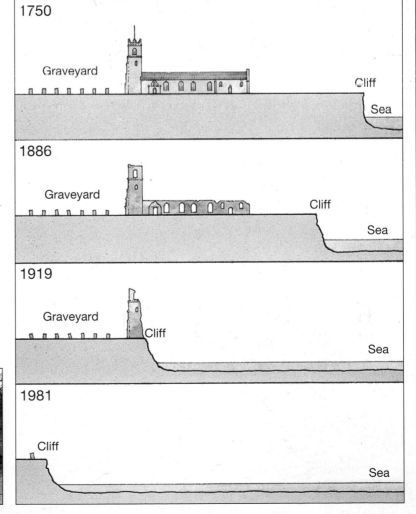

1750

Graveyard Cliff

Sea

1886

Graveyard Cliff

Sea

1919

Graveyard Cliff

Sea

1981

Cliff

Sea

Defending the Coastline

◀ This farmland in the Netherlands has been reclaimed from the sea. These areas are called **polders**. The land is fertile and flat.

● Defending the coast is expensive and can cause other problems. For example, using barriers, or groins, to prevent sand from moving along the shore may stop other sandy beaches from forming. Protecting cliffs from wave erosion stops pebbles and new sand forming from the rocks that fall away from cliffs.

People who live on the coast protect their shore from the sea in different ways. They may build sea walls to protect the roads and houses in seaside towns. Long earthen walls may keep the sea from flooding low-lying farmland. At many places along the coast, people plant pine trees or tough, quick-growing grasses with long roots, such as marram grass. The trees and plants trap the dry sand that blows from beaches. Blown sand often forms low hills called **sand dunes** above the high-tide level. The dunes will help protect the coast from damage during a storm.

In ports and harbors, stone or concrete walls called breakwaters shelter ships while they load and unload cargo and passengers. On beaches, or in the sea close by, there may be low walls called groins. They stop the waves from moving sand along the shore and protect the coast from erosion.

▼ These walls, or breakwaters, help shelter this old harbor at Caesarea in Israel. Beyond the walls, the sea is choppy and sometimes stormy. Inside the walls, the water stays calm. When the harbor was in use, the breakwater allowed boats to load and unload safely.

- About 20 percent of the land in the Netherlands has been reclaimed from the sea.

- Reclaiming land can have a bad effect on wildlife. Damming the Zuider Zee has destroyed the marshes where many plants, seabirds, wild ducks and geese once lived. The Dutch government has now decided to leave an area called Markerwaard as marshland. It is very rich in plants and wildlife.

Case Study

One country that has had to learn how to protect its coast against the sea is the Netherlands. Much of the land there is below sea level. Over hundreds of years, the Dutch people have built seawalls called **dikes** to stop the sea from flooding the land. They have also gradually reclaimed land from the sea. One example of this has been the damming of the bay called the Zuider Zee. Before the dam was built, Dutch engineers had to keep repairing the seawalls that protected almost 200 miles of winding coastline around this bay. After they built the dam, there were only 19 miles of seawall to repair. The salt water that the dam trapped in the bay was pumped out and rivers flowing into the bay eventually formed the freshwater Lake Ijssel.

Geography Detective

Look at the two maps. They show the Zuider Zee reclamation scheme in the Netherlands. Make a list of all the changes that have taken place since 1920. In what ways have these changes helped the Netherlands? Why is there a greater risk of flooding in the Netherlands than in many other countries?

▶ Maps of the Zuider Zee in 1920 and in 1990

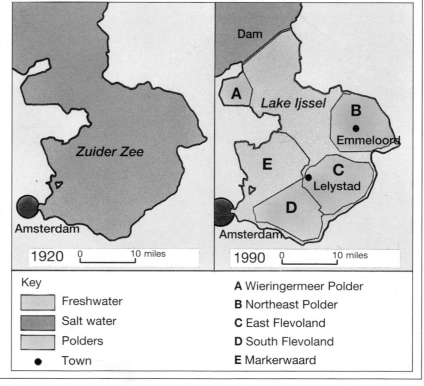

1920   0 —— 10 miles

1990   0 —— 10 miles

Key

▢	Freshwater
▢	Salt water
▢	Polders
●	Town

A Wieringermeer Polder
B Northeast Polder
C East Flevoland
D South Flevoland
E Markerwaard

How We Use Oceans and Seas

Oceans and seas provide us with many of our needs. They are highways for transporting goods and people, and they supply us with food and many raw materials for industries.

Fish are an important source of food. In countries such as Japan and Indonesia, people eat

◀ Some fish stocks are low because methods of fishing have changed. Many countries now use huge ships. They can travel very long distances and they use large nets that sweep up enormous numbers of fish in one catch.

▼ This beach on the coast of Brazil is a popular place for vacations. Tourist towns, or resorts, have grown up along many coasts, especially in places with fine beaches and warm weather. People like to swim or take part in water sports such as sailing and windsurfing.

Fish farms like this one in China can produce large numbers of fish. Local people can buy fresh fish, and the rest is frozen and sent away to be sold. Salmon and trout are examples of fish that can be farmed in this way. Many coastal places now have fish farms nearby.

far more fish than meat. Some types of animal feed and crop fertilizers contain fish. The world demand for fish has grown so much that stocks of some kinds of fish are declining. Many countries have had to agree on where they may fish and on how much they catch. When stocks of some species run low, the whole food chain is affected (see page 15).

Nearly half the world's oil and gas resources lie below the continental shelves. These supplies are tapped from oil platforms, or rigs. There are offshore oil fields near many coasts, including Alaska and Louisiana in the United States, Nigeria in Africa, and northwestern Europe.

Other seabed products are sands, gravels, and minerals such as copper and manganese. Seawater also contains useful chemicals.

● Potato-shaped balls, or nodules, containing metals such as copper have been discovered on the ocean bed at depths of 13,000 feet and more. If the price of metals rises, it may be worth the expense of collecting these in the future.

Geography Detective

Look back to pages 14 and 15 where you read about the food chain in the oceans. Why do you think it is important to control the number of fish caught? What can happen as a result of over fishing of some types of fish?

Poisoning the Water

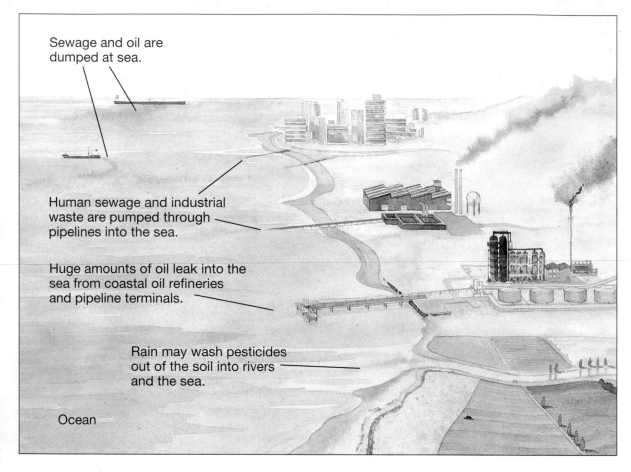

Sewage and oil are dumped at sea.

Human sewage and industrial waste are pumped through pipelines into the sea.

Huge amounts of oil leak into the sea from coastal oil refineries and pipeline terminals.

Rain may wash pesticides out of the soil into rivers and the sea.

Ocean

The oceans and seas are so vast that it is difficult to imagine that they can be poisoned, or polluted, by the wastes that are dumped into them. But they can. As the above diagram shows, most wastes are made on the land. For example, farmers use chemicals to kill crop pests, and rain washes these pesticides into rivers and out into the sea. Other wastes, such as oil, may spill into the sea by accident.

The result of all this pollution is that plants and animals that live in or near the sea can be harmed or killed. When one type of creature is harmed, others—including humans—may suffer, too.

Many countries are now working together to reduce sea pollution. Laws are being passed to stop the problem from getting worse.

▲ Many waste materials come from cities, towns, and farms near rivers and coasts. When waste reaches the sea, it can poison plants and animals living there. Pollution can also make it unsafe for humans to swim in the sea or to eat fish that come from contaminated waters.

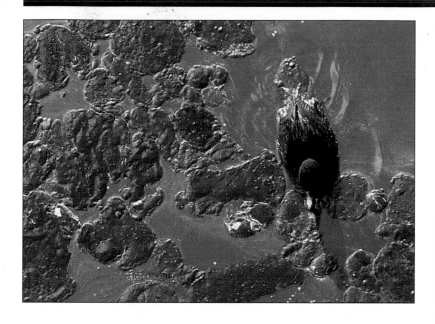

◄ This seabird is covered with crude oil. The oil spilled out of an oil tanker called the *Sea Empress* when it hit rocks near Milford Haven, Wales, in 1996.

● About 50 years ago, a Japanese factory dumped a dangerous chemical called methyl mercury into the sea. The mercury found its way into the flesh of the tuna fish. By 1975 more than 3,500 people had been poisoned or paralyzed as a result of eating the polluted fish.

Case Study

In 1989 the oil tanker *Exxon Valdez* struck a reef in Prince William Sound, Alaska. About 11 million gallons of crude oil spilled into the water. The disaster killed huge numbers of fish such as salmon and herring. More than 100,000 seabirds died, as well as seals, sea otters, and many other animals. Nearly 1,250 miles of coastline were polluted. It cost millions of dollars to clean the sea and the beaches. More than 10,000 people were involved in the rescue operation.

Geography Detective

What clues would you look for on a beach to tell you that it is polluted? Make a list of them. For each item on your list, think of a way to deal with this type of pollution.

◄ Sewage pollutes the sea at the port of Rio de Janeiro in Brazil.

Mapwork

The map on page 29 shows a small stretch of coastline with two towns, Puerta and Playa. Puerta is a fishing port, Playa is a seaside resort with hotels for visitors. Most of the people who live in these towns earn a living from fishing or tourism.

1. Use the scale on the map to find the distance a bird would fly in a straight line from Puerta to Playa.
2. Use the map scale and a length of string to measure the distance a fish would swim from Puerta to Playa, if it swam close to the shore. How much farther would the fish swim than the bird would fly?
3. Which town is further to the north, Puerta or Playa?
4. Make a copy of the map. Find the features on the map that are similar to those shown in the three photographs below. Write in the names of these features in the empty boxes A, B, and C on your map.
5. Mark your copy of the map with letters to show where you would see:
   a) a bay (mark it with the letter D)
   b) a harbor (mark it with the letter E)
   c) a headland (mark it with the letter F)
   d) people on a beach (mark it with the letter G)
   e) fishing boats (mark it with the letter H).
6. Write the following labels in the correct places on your copy of the map: lagoon, island, sandbar, strait.

A   B   C

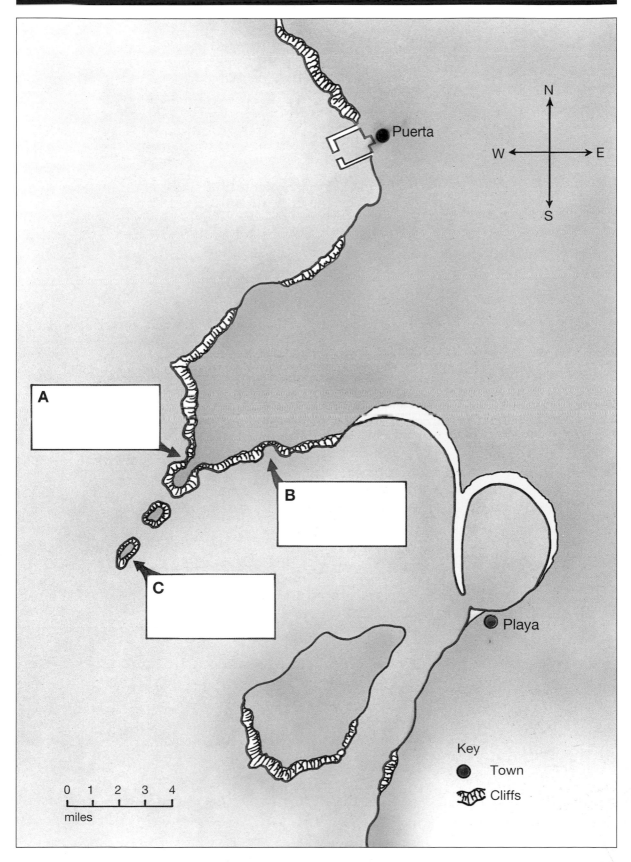

A

B

C

N
W   E
S

Puerta

Playa

Key

● Town

〰️ Cliffs

0   1   2   3   4
miles

Glossary

bay: A small part of an ocean or sea that forms in an indentation in the coastline.

continental shelf: The edge of a continent that is below sea level.

continental slope: The steep incline between the continental shelf and the ocean bed.

coral reef: A line of rocks or small islands made from the skeletons of millions of dead coral. Corals live in warm, tropical seas.

desalinization plant: A factory that turns salt water from the sea into freshwater.

dike: A seawall built to control flooding.

equator: The imaginary line drawn on maps around the center of the earth.

erode: To wear away earth or rocks, by the action of water, wind, or ice.

fetch: The distance traveled by waves without interruption.

food chain: A series of plants and animals, each of which is a source of food for the next member in the web.

gulf: A section of ocean or sea that extends into land.

headland: A piece of land sticking out into the sea.

hurricane: A very strong wind that originates over the ocean and can cause severe damage.

lagoon: An area of shallow water separated from the open sea by reefs, sandbars, or sandbanks.

longshore drift: An action of the waves that moves sand and mud along the shore.

neap tides: The lowest tides of the month.

ocean bed: The land surface at the bottom of the ocean.

ocean current: A movement of water through an ocean. Currents are caused mainly by winds and are often near the ocean surface.

peninsula: Meaning "almost an island," a piece of land that extends into the sea.

phytoplankton: Plants of the plankton group that are moved in water by waves or currents.

plankton: Minute plants and creatures that live close to the surface of the sea. They provide food for fish.

polder: A piece of low land reclaimed from the sea.

sand dune: A large bank of sand, piled up by the wind.

sandbar: A long bank of sand deposited by the sea. It may block the mouth of a river or the entrance to a bay.

sea: A body of salt water surrounded on two or three sides by land.

spring tides: The highest tides of the month.

stack: A tall piece of rock in the sea. It stands a few yards away from the cliffs from which it was eroded.

strait: A narrow channel of water that links one sea to another or to an ocean.

tide: The twice-daily rise and fall in sea level.

trench: A very deep channel in the bed of the ocean. A trench may be hundreds or even thousands of yards deep.

tsunami: A huge ocean wave that is caused by an underwater earthquake or volcano.

volcano: A place where gases and melted rock explode through the surface, or crust, of the earth. As the rock cools, it forms a hill or mountain. Some islands are volcanoes that rise above the surface of the sea.

wave-cut platform: A platform of bare rock left behind when the waves erode a sea cliff.

zooplankton: Animals of the plankton group that can move themselves in water.

METRIC CONVERSION CHART		
WHEN YOU KNOW	**MULTIPLY BY**	**TO FIND**
inches	25.4	millimeters
inches	2.54	centimeters
feet	0.3048	meters
miles	1.609	kilometers
square miles	2.59	square kilometers
acres	0.4047	hectares
gallons	3.78	liters
degrees Fahrenheit	.56 (after subtracting 32)	degrees Celsius

Index

adaptation to the environment 17
anglerfish 17
arch 18, 19
Arctic Ocean 4, 5
Atlantic Ocean 5, 7, 10

Bangladesh 11, 20, 21
bay 4, 5, 19, 23, 28
Bay of Bengal 4, 11
beach 22, 24, 27, 28

Caspian Sea 4
channel 6, 8
cliff 18, 19, 20, 22
continental shelf 6, 8, 14, 25
continental slope 6
coral 9, 15
current 10, 12, 19
cyclone 10

desalinization plant 9
dike 23
Dunwich 21

equator 5, 10
erosion 19, 20, 22
evaporation 8, 9, 10
Exxon Valdez 27

fetch 12
fish farm 25
fishing 24, 25, 28
floods 11, 20, 21, 22, 23
food chain 15, 25

groin 22
gulf 4, 5, 10, 11
Gulf of Mexico 4, 10
Gulf Stream 10, 11
gulper eel 16

hatchet fish 16
headland 5, 28
hurricane 10, 11

Ijssel, Lake 23
Indian Ocean 5, 6

Krakatoa 20

Labrador Current 10
lagoon 19, 28
lantern fish 17
longshore drift 19

Mediterranean Sea 4

Netherlands 20, 22, 23
North Atlantic Ocean 7, 10

ocean bed 6, 7, 16, 17, 25
oil 6, 25, 26, 27

Pacific Ocean 5, 7, 11, 16, 20
peninsula 5
Peru current 10
plankton 14, 15
polders 22
pollution 26, 27

red tide 15

salt 8, 9
sandbar 19, 28
seabed 6, 19, 20, 25
sewage 27
shellfish 9, 15
species 14, 25
stack 18, 19
strait 4, 5, 28

tidal power station 13
tide 12, 13, 18, 19, 21, 22
trench 6, 7
tsunami 20
tuna 15, 27
typhoon 10, 21

viper fish 16
volcano 6, 17

wave power 13
wave-cut platform 18, 19
whale 14

Zuider Zee 23